AVA Ascent, LLC

www.avaaction.com

The first step of

change

*is to become aware
of your own*

[**bullshit.**]

Reflecting on the past can jumpstart our progress forward.

Stop and take a deep dive on the past year. This journal provides a simple life assessment along with 50 reflection prompts to create a recap of the past 12 months.

Save favorite memories, reflect on changes in your life, and assess your self-development.

Write as much or little as you like. Once completed, you'll have an overview of the year to save as a diary, as well as inspiration to set new goals for your life moving forward.

Enjoy!

Team AVA
avaaction.com

YEAR

GET STARTED

Grab any calendars, planners, and photos from the past year
that can help you remember what happened the past 12 months.

LIFE ASSESSMENT

On a scale from 1-10, 1 being low,
rate how well each area of your life went this past year.

HEALTH	
Mind	
Body	
Heart	

CAREER	
Work / School	
Personal Development	
Volunteering	

HOUSEKEEPING	
Homecare	
Financial	
Food	

RELATIONSHIPS	
Family	
Friends	
Significant Other	

FUN	
Hobbies	
Vacation	
Entertainment	

1

If someone wrote a book about my life this past year, what kind of genre would it be?

(A comedy, love story, drama, film noir or something else?)

2

What or who had the largest positive impact
on my life this past year?

3

What are 3 highlights of my past year?

4

What are 3 low points of my past year?

5

Looking back on this past year I feel...

6

A year ago today, I...

7

What one event, big or small, am I going to tell my grandchildren about?

8

I never thought I would...

What was my favorite place I visited?

What was my favorite place I visited?

10

Best news I received?

11

Favorite compliment I received?

12

Best gift I received?

13

Funniest moment of the year, one that still makes it hard
not to burst out laughing?

14

What purchase turned out to be the best decision ever?

15

What did I do on my birthday?

16

This past year, I've become addicted to...

17

My biggest adventure this year was...

18

Favorite Quote(s) from this year:

19

What personal goals or habits did I accomplish?

20

This year I focused most of my time on...

My most rewarding moment was when...

22

The biggest obstacles I faced were...

23

What new strategies or tools helped my productivity?

24

What helped me focus the most?

25

I'm disappointed that I didn't...

26

What is still making me feel stuck?

27

I'm still terrified of...

28

If I could, what advice would I give myself
at the beginning of this past year?

at the beginning of this past year?

29

Who was my number one go-to person
that I could always rely on?

30

What 5 people did I most enjoy spending time with?

31

How did my relationship with family evolve?

32

What was my favorite moment spent with friends?

How satisfied am I with the relationships I'm trying to build?

34

Is there any anger towards anyone I need to let go of
before I move forward in life?

35

Is there anyone I need to forgive?

36

Do I need to forgive myself for anything?

37

What new things did I discover about myself this year?

38

Which of my personal qualities turned out to be
the most helpful this year?

Which worries turned out to be completely unnecessary?

40

I was naive thinking...

41

What patterns of negative-self talk emerged this year?

42

What do I need to heal in my life?

What is holding me back?

44

What do I spend a silly amount of money on?

45

Was there anything I did for the very first
time in my life this year?

46

The biggest lesson I learned was...

47

How am I different today from a year ago?

48

I've become really passionate about...

49

How did my overall outlook on life evolve?

50

Did any parts of myself do a complete 180 this year?

Say farewell to this year!

If there is anything else left that you'd like to write down,
or any person you need further closure with,
do it now!